# THE COMMERCE BETWEEN TONGUES

**adrija ghosh** is a polyglot poet, translator, and filmmaker who talks a lot about love and a lot about loneliness. she travels the world along with her political, flaneur lyric-'i'. you might bump into her in an airport, an art gallery, or a bookshop. otherwise, you can find her on twitter and instagram at @byadrija.

ISBN: 978-1-915760-21-0

The author has asserted their right to be identified as the author of this Work in accordance with the Copyright, Designs and Patents Act 1988

Cover designed by Aaron Kent

Edited & Typeset by Aaron Kent

Broken Sleep Books Ltd
Rhydwen
Talgarreg
Ceredigion
SA44 4HB

Broken Sleep Books Ltd
Fair View
St Georges Road
Cornwall
PL26 7YH

# the commerce between tongues

*adrija ghosh*

Broken Sleep Books

# Contents

# বাগী/*bari*/বাড়ি[1]

the human mouth is briefly lamentable
after a night of giving birth to grief
which is real tragedy which is counterfeit?

am i prometheus
because you stole the sun

cracked it
open
on the poplar tree
outside your liberton road window
the yellow yolk dripped on the tip of the tree
and autumn made attendance

i might be prometheus
because cirrhosis runs in my family.

i must have inherited bad genes as well as a bleeding bank account

my liver,
an hors d'oeuvre
a western metaphor for premature deaths and dislocation
from north calcutta একান্নবর্তী² families
to small town rehabs to funeral pyres at twenty.

if reincarnation is omnipresence of pain
then the world is what maa claims it to be -
furniture fold
house plants,
an armchair view of the sea from colaba,
an economy of desire
marked by the will to touch-grief-tragedy

an open lease.

on the day i was born,
maa did not go into labour.
in her womb i rotated somehow,
almost drowned, tasted the amniotic
she bloated instead, trying
to keep me afloat
i still feel guilty
for the scissor marks on her body.

maa named me
on the operation table, knowing
this name would one day be a stamp inside a passport jacket.

in her
foresight, i
was already
exiled.

bengali households name you twice:
hard eyed,
quick teethed,
dried crunchy kale, on most paperwork

soft bellied
semolina-custard
nickname
coconut oiled on summer days:


                                              my name,

                           a

movie

                  in

jump

                              cut.

my body, brown

a playground
for melanin politics

battered in beds
where often sex
is a patriarchal discourse
a geopolitical nuisance.


(and, they all want me to love my body)

but i have grown sick

|          |       | of  |         | loving |
|          |       |     |         | bodies, |
| cities   | made  | of  |         | bodies, |
| sickness | made  | of  |         | bodies, |
| love     | made  | of  |         | bodies; |

love, doesn't make the body.

on nights when baba makes obscure bangla literary references to
সুহাসিনীর পমেটম by কমলকুমার মজুমদার  a novel without
punctuation maa fears that i have started to mourn in devanagari
memory is substratal and maa does not know how to console my
polyglot grief i wonder if bangla without the oxford comma is what
my inner monologue should be i have hence found all synonyms
for abandonment and reduced them to a ten-milligram dosage of
escitalopram my sad white deus ex machina wrapped in foil the
only habit i remember not to break


within the body

grief is without

punctuation

never

pausing

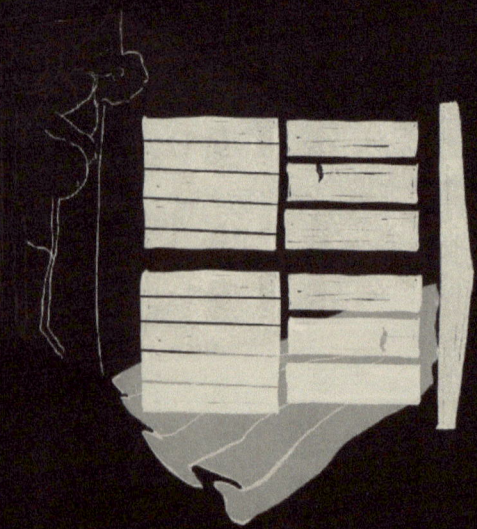

                              a seance for my friend.
dead at twenty-five.
too much meth in his veins, not enough jaggery.


a december baby.
upon birth, he was fed sugar stirred coconut.
every birthday, hence, he awaited my return from darjeeling.
"mimi, first. then, cake."


and i was only seventeen, when he said he loved me.


and i need to believe he is dead, maa.
he won't ever look at me, hidden behind memories.


are these my roots, maa- cirrhosis, drug abuse, fiscal debt, abortions?

the empty nest syndrome i gifted my parents at fifteen
when i moved out from our ghost town to a crumbling north-
calcutta address
squeezed me
into a matchbox housing penury.
a pigeonhole, where dreams are euthanized; where white termites
eat books to survive.

i was eight, still in primary,
home alone when the news arrived
my uncle was dead because his liver exploded
i was twenty-two, when my friend shrunk
his beard still soft as plume, unshaved
a sparrow amidst twigs.

all funeral pyres look like empty nests, ever since.

the grandfather clock above his bed swung our childhood with
each strike –
he didn't wake up, he didn't wake up, he didn't wake up,
he wouldn't respond, he wouldn't respond, he wouldn't respond.

the next day,
i took a flight out of the country
and spent a year in exile.

is pity a human symptom, is mythmaking?

a city is a fortuity waiting to happen.

during my end days
in edinburgh, i stayed with an aging actor.
to him, home was a fifth-floor apartment in leith.
there was a black & white photograph of an ex-lover from forty
years ago
perched on a giant piano, his ex: a travolta look alike.
he, sixty: eating soup from tupperware, watching jeopardy.

i never asked,
why the memorabilia?
why the keepsake of heartbreak?
why the dust on the piano?

during the pandemic,
breaking the fourth wall
the city spoke to me through windows

i bought postcards to optimize my experience
city-window-home
a soundbite, a teaser
to preserve tartan, titian, tattie scones
to discard pavements, cobblestones, john kay at west bow
to decide - this must stay, this must go
to decide - this is worth customs; this is worth cultural currency.

do you still like your eggs runny?
two golden suns over easy tuesday afternoon brunch rituals
overlooking the milky gossamer fog which engulfs delhi
every day at breakfast, i remember wrists scrambling eggs
in our friend's apartment at gk
in delhi the metro spins around the city: a string of marigold disrupting
air pollution and a kiss
in sanjay's van i thought was affection which made my respiration
laboured and not red flags beeping through air purifiers.
in edinburgh, on days you are lucky the sun punctures the mist
in delhi's *kohara* becomes sea-fret becomes 'haar' to the scots, it
spins a spider web around kirkyards and traps the city
in gothic whispers. summer hill at shimla, haymarket near dalry –
stations often blur
into a singular quick stopover at queen street or nizamuddin.

it might be the river
which has flown
through tudor bloodlines literary cycles carrying
tax, trade routes, refugees,
but the city moves and moves and moves

a dancer bending her body in tulle –
london is a city in constant motion.
                              but
you can't exactly pre-rehearse farewells for a city

(cities are lovers too.)

i odyssey the sea
five times in eleven months.
homesickness is not dialectical; there is no purpose, no virtue
                                                      to voyage.

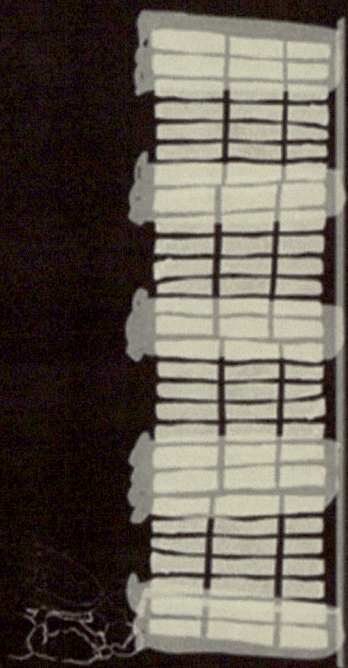

belongingness is an invocation of violence.

*humara koi sheher nahi,*
so we can belong to neighbourhoods, bookstores, mouths, beds
and claim: belonging to a postal address is to never belong at all.

we transform into polycultural maps where we are nobodies
without bodies still aspiring for self-hood.
in postmemory, there is no self-actualization because i don't ever
want to know the person i am, i was, i can't be.

belongingness becomes an inquiry –
a keyword in a statement of intent
a perpetual city in motion
a room in a north calcutta house eaten alive by termites.

once you live out of suitcases,
in airports in constant motion sickness in neither here never there-
you stop befriending familiar faces from capital cities
who think motion is vacation,
or worse, vocation.

and roots,
wretched roots,
heavy excuse for stasis.

a sarcophagus,
a receptacle for a tourist in transit;
history is unmoved.

the myth goes,
when jahangir fell in love with mumtaz,
he sent an army to this town
they killed sher afghan while he was offering namaz,
and ever since we house ghost narratives of betrayal.

if fate is circular,
then the spinnerets in this town crochet stories
of maternal neglect, property dispute, sibling rivalry, and land
mutation: seismic waves of middle-class strife.

december daybreaks are occupied by flowery orange pekoe from the
lopchu tea estate.
i slip into the hanging window at my grandmother's. she snores, the
money plant whirrs in the breeze.
men from all around town come to the palatial pink house opposite
ours, around the clock they process coal.
i assist her. at seventy-five, she has allowed
her palms to merge knife skills and osteoporosis into chiromancy.
she kneads fennel and peeled peas into the dough.

and tradition is a poltergeist serving us dinner.

খিড়কী/*khirki*/খিড়কি³

চাঁদে একটা মস্ত বড় বাগানবাড়ি আছে,
আছে নারকেল গাছে বোনা ঘুড়ি
আছে তোর আমার খোলা খিড়কি।⁴

in hindi khirki means জানালা⁵ //
in bangla খিড়কি means a postern
(a guerilla exit)

you pack your bags// i skip town
we hover//you haunt

(i defer arrivals)

my childhood//a tarmac
of unceasing departure//i keep
bidding you goodbye//you keep biding time

traced back to c.1200
window (n.)
festers in old norse
"vindauga"//or, "wind-eye"

i say চোখ⁶//you are six feet under
etymology points
to an "eye-door"// alternatively, a "breath-door"
i choke on the word breath
i search violently for you in the dark

(you say *yok*⁷ and you mean eyes
i say yoke, and i too, mean eyes.

yours.)

## summer

lolls over like a wet tongue from a wet dog. i watch maa

hunched over the sink. she is scaling fish head with a steel spoon.
the scales shimmer

in the morning light. sweat sticks to her nape.

the air is heavy with jackfruit flesh making its way into curries.

my memory is a morgue. my childhood empty

except for the solitary kite string that tugs and tugs and tugs until
it snaps.

the steel in maa's hand makes ugly red indentations into her skin,

and for a moment i wonder

if this domestic docility will end up drawing blood.

the rain never stops in august.

it is vicious,
    vicious,
    vicious. my grief

does not see the face of the sun. it turns inside my stomach like
sunflowers.

turns towards its only source of light – my open mouth in mourning.

the sun rises ripe ramen red in front of my window,

and earthen mortal men are flying into space wearing jumbo white suits.

i want to ask them if they see you tying kites to saturn's rings.

i want to ask you, is it lonely up there?

you tell me: bumps on the moon is flesh, and flesh alone in rot.

maa tells me: fate is newton's third law of motion and i believe her. i beg,

quit the spoon, walk away from it.

towards what? you challenge.

you are dead. i wait.

# *grief is my houseguest.*

we sit on our floor mats
we break
bread for dinner.

she tells me a story —
a deer caught
surprised.

grief finishes
my bread first
then she reaches for my rice.

asks me,
ever wonder
how far you had to come
to end up here —
at the roadside

waiting
like a predestined
roadkill
surprised
to be skirted around
and not run over?

she squabbles, i starve.

in her hands, soil
tastes like carrots.
in my hunger, no animosity
is worth rotting meat.

we squabble, i squander.

grief is here
to consecrate
the god-shaped hole in my heart.

अतिथिदेवो भव [8]

## "for my grandfather's funeral, we offered cigarettes"

the birds: art brut.
they flock against a toothpaste sky.
i long to go back to cramond. watch the sea disappear.
i think a lot about death. i am scared it might hurt.

20,000 courtesans from yoshiwara's harem were enshrined and
given flowers.
"flower rondeau" (1997) - a "flower-fuck scene".
bodies splayed flat still.
lizard king. basquait. japanese prostitutes. dubuffet.
lonely rimbaud haunting nyc.
death by syphilis at 23. death by meth at 25.
eros-youth-decay.

i carry you.
perpetual urn in my arms.
across dining tables, swimming lessons, bookstores.
aftertaste of daulat ki chaat.
you weigh heavy on my tongue.
the weather is a recipe. apparition clouds. plastic trees.
the kitchen smells like holly if holly smelt like curry powder.
christmas is here.
i long to go back to cramond. walk on water.
bring you back to life.

eat well.[9]

# বারি[10]

i.      in my grief, i turn into a rhinoceros.
          i lick my wounds like salt.

ii.     i grew up beside a canal.
          i have known floods since i was born.
          water eats my house.

iii.    i am not scared of water – just the amniotic.

iv.    one time, i tell him i never want children. he challenges –
          "i can't wait to impregnate you."
          i am an indigo farmer, ploughing my body, begging it to
          be infertile. just in case.

v.      ganga. thames.
          ahiritola. anglia.
          ouroboros.
          i am charnock on a raft.

          this is where i moor.

vi.    the chandipur beach near bhubaneswar recedes 5 km
          twice a day.
          it reminds me of cramond.
          the sea doesn't dare come close.
          we sit on wet sand, and i don't want him coming close.

vii.   "i had to put a continent and the north sea between us
          maa otherwise i would have never escaped."

viii.     i am not scared to try again. "you could be," my therapist
muses, "that is your trauma response.
people react differently to abuse." a diagnosis, fear of
abandonment, ptsd.
my grief on an open table.

ix.     therapy helps. i take it with a pinch of salt.

x.     saltwater can be disinfectant on the right tongue.
come over. wipe me clean.

# guldasta[11]

*khuab mein tum shehzada, safed ghori, shayari*
*galat uljhi main, mujhe urdu tak nehi aati[12]–*

all songs are part-time lullabies under open skies in montgomery park
i take a loop around the royal mile at midnight

stolen milk tastes better in chai
maybe i should have stolen a taste of you
frieda kahlo in a saree
the first time i saw you
you knotted your eyes at the sun
unibrow
collarbone
starched shirt
kohlapuris

maybe, i fell in love?

*mere purane se sheher mein na lehrey hai na tere lafz*
*phir bhi kuch khat hain[13]*
but if you roll your vowels round like i do
then in bengali ক্ষত[14] means a wound
a paper cut at bahrisons–

অধরা[15] *adhoora shaam[16]*
eight pm clouds over arthur's seat like scratches on an old begum
akhtar record
that tune which you hummed
that tune which stayed on my tongue like a cigarette burn
that ghazal about moonlight skipping town
leaving you  wanting
                waiting

*galat uljhi main, mujhe raatbhar neend tak nehi aati*[17]-


you spoke in wet spots and prodigal fingers, crocheting my skin
with needles sharper than my tongue,
stinging more than my pride,
clinging to my breath, your words
power cuts in late july
with thunderstorms and lukewarm laal chai, summers
in new york, blistering
sea salt soft jazz with clothes off


nowadays the pandemic pattern looks like your hip bones in high
waisted jeans a dostoevsky hiccup from a girl
in love in a russian city


*ek* marlboro *ka dabba*[18],
my friends and i used to fill champagali
with smoke honey sticks cold white anger
when the white frangipanis bloomed
in the late summer of twenty-nineteen,
we weren't there. but i remember
you reading rilke,
lifting a flower from the road, tucking it behind my ear.


*kaash woh guldasta humara bhi hota –*[19]


i would trade all the amaltas of delhi,
the spring and the aandhi,
to walk with you
in our old college campus
*galat uljhi main, tumhe meri yaad tak nehi aati–*[20]

# *can you smell a memory in vacuum?*

66.25 million years ago,
volcanoes erupted at the western ghats
so i could light a candle and bottle you up in the deccan trap:
i must remember how you smelled that day –
you, in your white helmet and green sweater,
it was spring in edinburgh: confetti of blossoms.
your hair catching dew sloshing against my palms in waves
you you you
you laughed at our legs entangled in the north sea at portobello. said:
*iss ghair mulk mein mohabbat na kar baithe hum.*[21]
i saw faces of poets who were refugees within their motherland
                                                    their mothertongue.


after you left, you sent a postcard: a picture of the bass rock.
we were northern gannets, perched on volcanic cliffs overlooking
the berwick island.
your body: a paperweight, holding me down after breakfast.
we watched petal dance from your kitchen countertop and
discussed chekov.
you said, russian authors could sense god.


on liberton windows water froze
in tiger prints, i
excavated the tip of your tongue from double decker duvets:
a morsel of affection; cross-border dole during thundersnow in
scotland.
you filled your cycle basket with funeral flowers – daisies, rowan
berries
said, this is how you must imagine me: *laal*[22] paneer, scrabble in
direct sunlight, lips
rattling in sleep, tiptoes on your bathroom tile breaking the surface
tension of should i leave or should i stay.

in my arms, you spoke in closed captions. shoved your language in
my mouth
on surface level, tongue became language.
your head, cumulonimbus clouds, a forest of fern in darjeeling, the
first sip of oolong.
your mouth, proper poetry: brined in languages inviting censorship,
obscenity trials and sedition in my country

*aajkal iss mulk mein ishq bhi inquilab hai.*[23]

*aren't museums lonely places?*

nobody comes to art galleries to collect sadness
the recollection of sorrow is always remembered more than grief
itself.

# সোনার বাগান

*meri pyaari* [24]mina revelled in her flower crown
cream and peaches, at her *dua-e-khair*[25], she braided রজনীগন্ধা[26]
and roses in her hair, and i have been thinking about my
grandmother since. every evening
over her cup of *laal chaa*[27], didai sits with her old wedding album.
her skin, sepia moth eaten চন্দন[28]; dadu perhaps ten years elder; in
memory, still alive.


didai received lots of gold. a list could be made of fifty-seven items:
earrings necklace bangles anklets nose-pins rings.
none remain, not a single drop of yellow. she sold most of it to feed
communist rebels
pay her sister-in-law's dowry
she gave away a bulky pair of bracelets so that my youngest
grandfather could stay in school
she could not wear rings while cooking fuel out of dung
so she sold them to the goldsmith knitting her family tighter, some
ungrateful
amnesiac hundred –


the album shows most souvenirs, but the legendary one is missing.
the mythical **সোনার বাগান**[29] – hair about her shoulder, gilded gold
i imagine what it must have looked like,


the taxi yellow against her ivory forehead,
her ivory tower, her ivory fate


chashma shahi, eden in twenty-four carats
golden garden for her thick black hair
*kaash woh guldasta humara bhi hota-*[30]

40

## afsana [31]

the post-colonial conspiracy convinces
us that trains are essential
(vehicles of violence, vehicles of separation)
a colonial boon *if*
we find lovers in compartments-

on such a train
station in october –

(have you noticed all my favourite love stories start near a ten fifteen
to manali or vienna or king's cross
a last goodbye from a broken boy, seventeen, weeping; *palat*[32];
restlessness, fear – what if this train doesn't stop for me for you for
the liminal destination we call fate?
if you get on this train/if you get off this train
"*daal chawal* for 50 *saal* till you die"[33]
in eight years i will miss the plane and you
can sing me a tune; julie delpy impersonating nina simone in paris,
movie actor in isolation, death by stroke
in october - we stirred; red, blue, incidental.)

i draped a white cotton saree
and you peeled the kalamkari off my chest
leaned against the white wall.

we drew borders with our bodies
thread counts of ceasefires.

underdeveloped aversion to your open mouth i wanted to put a lid
on it
and throw dirt.

six feet under, between enemy lines-
i tugged at your muscle memory into a half-drunk smile
glitched when i caught your eyes.

you stood
counting minimizing
spectral measurements distance pragmatism
one step forward two steps back
a cadence not meant for us

i chase moments
my brief romance is with
the unfulfilled,
the let's-make-a-move,
one way ticket to glasgow-lyon-bangalore
i spend my life perfecting goodbyes.

*par ye rozana lamho mein na tumhara alvida tha na tumhare sheher ka pata*[34]
you left me
with a memory
a camping trip
the isle of skye
a promise
of yellow gorse
gleaming like flashlights from tourists in the city
september in edinburgh - red, blue, purple

heather flowers
a double rainbow over lyne
(*kaash woh guldasta humara bhi hota*)[35]

in my grasp,
for the first time
stubborn at the face of joy

impractical desire
*mulmul*[36]

fifteen questions, intense eye contact, two pall malls-
the first night we met you plunged
from the hilltop into the reservoir
a sprig of rosemary in sun melted butter
in my freezing palms
*mulmul*

your eyes fixed me
an evening drink
a drop of red in room temperature
a wisp of touch
touch everywhere
*tumhari nazr ko koi tou roke*[37]

your mouth,
always open in protest.
*ek kafir fasana*[38]- "here is my light, here is my hand, i don't bite but i
am a believer."
your mouth,
always soft, a question mark
fixed noiselessly on mine
*mulmul*

you don't stop, you don't stare, you hardly look.
an open casket burial for my affection
which you think
is sorrow
and kiss away
at waverley

you freeze me
in the in-between
between picket fence and barbed wires -

*(kaash woh jannat humein bhi naseeb hota)*[39]

# *Wisteria in Spring*

it rains mid-afternoon, uncharacteristic of delhi.
i have a plane to catch (the first of many).
we watch *pakeezah* in bed; meena kumari dancing
in a pink palatial mansion, she moves
like water drop on a lotus leaf. her body
smeared in henna green, her eyes, **wisteria in spring**;
i remember
thinking *medusa nautchgirl.* we are both young,
pious, foolishly stir-crazy in my small bed. i am drying
my hair. it is two pm in delhi. you are walking
with your kohlapuris in hand.
i am late for a lecture in the journalism building.
you move
your tongue in sugar-coat on ten thousand places none of them
dreams all of them one single mouthful
of this drowsy afternoon.

we were not lovers. and i am stuck
in dubai during a layover. someone in queue is a whiff of wistful. you
are more myth than memory.

in g.k. does the rain still reek of you?
did you finally learn how to do laundry?

will you tuck a kiss between my toes?                          wait
for me-

                                                                ?

tonight, the moon
hangs in the sky, a solitary ফানুস[40] over the curzon gate.

a lone ranger lighting up the ranigunj bazaar *chowmatha.*[41]
the train rattles through this sleepy silent town.
instinctively, i find myself leaving you
for glasgow.

*baby, do you hear the train?*
mine or yours? it is just a train stop away.
central station? the green one?
king's cross, platform eleven –

do you think the greatest love stories which are never written- (*oh,
like mine and yours?*)
always begin, pause, and end on a rail-track?

no need to go down.
no need for movement.
*baby, you are always moving.*

*baby, i am moving away.*

if i am not leaving, i am lonely.
if i stay, i am stuck.

## *tonight i feel like my last lover.*

i want to touch my forehead against yours and breathe in years,
because time almost always smells like your winter jacket catching
snow in new york city.
cider, cedar wood and november in libraries.

beneath the poetry section,
wedged between mallarme and the sanitizer dispenser,
you were discussing cervantes with your friends in castilian,
and i could make out familiar words - spanish is phonetic, regional;
shakira, introductory lessons during third year of college, soap
operas.

in a community,
language is signifiers borrowed from each household.
in calcutta rooftops,
language is just an excuse to dissolve at touch, and mouths which
falter on saturdays.

you paused twice, i faltered.
frozen, perceived.
my hands traced the spine of an untranslated heptameron at till's,
your eyes, traffic lights;
slow yellow, deadpanning me red.
you look at me. you don't see through,
you don't accidentally brush past:
you hold my gaze.
i look away.

the moon makes an appearance,
i rehearse goodbyes.
behind the bass rock, the moon costs £1.45; one-way memorabilia

for a brief second beneath the poetry section wedged between
phonology and passport jackets,
uninterrupted debates on quixote,
(the rest simply noise)
the city, the traffic, the language;
just two strangers trying
not to break eye contact.

does gaze return gaze?
is it better to hold you instead?

tonight, i feel like my last lover.
when we almost bartered coffee for skin,
and the claustrophobia of calcutta kept me distracted,
as we dug into french toast at fransizka's.
in the kitchen, maa wants to bake milk into domesticity,
she boils palm sap for dessert.
i want to kiss the past.
i want to hold your mouth in my palms and drink you for dinner.

## sarson ka khet

so here we are,
in my one true metaphor for desire.
here is the yellow,
here is the movie script,
here we are,

looking at mustard fields and dreaming of love.

*sarson ka khet*, or nothing.

# *a bookmark is a repeat visit.*

you fold my skin into corners.
now, i am a dog-eared excuse of a lover.

home is a repeat visit.
so is a gallery at holyrood.
habit, history, visitor.
i look at art to look away from home(?)
under fiber-optic linear lamps,
my solitude (self portrait, oil on canvas)
is both holy and hollow.

nietzsche calls the moon a tomcat on the roof and dearest of
thieves you entered my terrace and gouged
out my eyes and i stopped seeing for myself. you picked up my
eyeball like a fish head in your mouth

i swayed in waves
desire
was high tide
was entrails of the moon
was its intestines and innards
was your hand on my wrist-
was a noose around the butterfly effect
of what could have been

there's a saying in edinburgh, in the local cognate dialect: "once you
kiss me, you cannot unkiss me."

vortex of arms and limbs, fragments, and mistaken chances
one more look at you before leaving.
one more.
one more.
one more.

# *Endnotes*

1    ঘারী – window in Punjabi.  বাড়ি – house/home in Bengali Both are pronounced bari.

2    একান্নবর্তী - joint family that shares one kitchen

3    খিড়কি – backdoor in Bengali, pronounced khirki

4    In moon, there is a country house. There is a kite hemmed into a coconut tree. There is our open khirki.

5    জানালা – window in Bengali

6    চোখ – eye(s) in Bengali, pronounced almost as choke

7    Yok – eye in Roma.

8    one for whom the guest is God.

9    usually in hindu funerals (shradhho), food is offered to the departed during the ritual of pindodaan.

10   বারি – Water in Bengali, pronounced bari.

11   In Urdu, guldasta means a bouquet of flowers, similar to the etymological origin of the word 'anthology', i.e., a collection of poems, which is derived from the Greek anthos "a flower" + legein "gather"
     (https://www.etymonline.com/word/anthology).

12   In my dreams/fantasies, you are a prince on a white horse. You are shayari, and it was my mistake to get tangled up, considering I don't even know Urdu.

13   In my aged city, there are neither waves nor your words, but there are a few letters,

14   Wound, pronounced khat-o, as opposed to khat.

15   অধরা – untouched in Bengali, pronounced o-dhora

16   Incomplete evening.

17   It was my mistake to get tangled up, considering I cannot sleep.

18   A packet of Marlboro.

19   I wish that guldasta were mine.

20   It was my mistake to get tangled up, considering you don't remember me.

21   I hope I don't fall in love in a foreign country.

22   red

23    Nowadays in this country love is revolution.

24    beloved

25    A ceremony where you bless the to be married couple.

26    রজনীগন্ধা – tuberose in Bengali

27    Black tea, although laal means red.

28    চন্দন – sandalwood in Bengali

29    সোনার বাগান – golden garden, ornamental comb in Bengali

30    I wish that guldasta were mine.

31    In Urdu it means a story, here a fairy tale.

32    Dilwale Dulhania Le Jayenge (1995)

33    Yeh Jawaani Hai Deewani (2013)

34    In these mundane moments, there was neither your farewell nor your postcode.

35    I wish I too was fated for flowers.

36    A fabric.

37    Someone should stop your gaze.

38    Your tongue was deceiving.

39    I wish I too was fated for such a paradise.

40    Paper lantern

41    Junction or roundabout.

# Acknowledgements

For all my ink and verse, I must pause and thank those who have unfurled their kindness and support, emboldening me to share my poetry. 'the commerece between tongues' is a reflection of our collective effort and I am grateful for each and every one of you. This poetry book is a tribute to you.

To Maa and Babai. My perfect parents, I love you.

To my editor, Aaron Kent, a tireless champion of my craft, for guiding me through moments of creative wear and tear. Thank you for giving my first collection a home in Broken Sleep Books.

To JK. For the art for 'baari'. For coparenting my brainchildren. For everything.

To my beautiful, funny friends who recognized me as a poet and an artist, long before I did. Across Calcutta, Dilli, Edinburgh, London, New York. Across time zones. Across divisions and differences. Across Foreign Policies and Border Controls – I hope we never lose sight of the community we have built.

To my community, the wind beneath my wings. Thank you.

To my peers and professors in Lady Shri Ram College, The University of Edinburgh, and the University of East Anglia. For educating, workshopping, and loving me into a better writer.

To the vibrant literary community. To *Gutter, The Dark Horse Magazine, bath magg,* and *No Contact Magazine* for unveiling early versions of some of these poems. To all the literary platforms that offered a platform for some of my other first drafts. Your recognition and appreciation gave me the courage to continue my craft.

To Bittu. Rest easy, old friend. I hope you never run out of kites to fly.

And to you – my reader. Walk with me. Let's walk for a long time. You found me. Thank You.

# LAY OUT YOUR UNREST

www.ingramcontent.com/pod-product-compliance
Lightning Source LLC
Chambersburg PA
CBHW041524090426
42737CB00038B/114